BLUE BANNER
BIOGRAPHY

Robert
DOWNEY JR.

Amie Jane Leavitt

Mitchell Lane
PUBLISHERS
P.O. Box 196
Hockessin, Delaware 19707
Visit us on the web: www.mitchelllane.com
Comments? email us: mitchelllane@mitchelllane.com

Mitchell Lane

PUBLISHERS

Printing   1   2   3   4   5   6   7   8   9

Blue Banner Biographies

Alicia Keys	Gwen Stefani	Megan Fox
Allen Iverson	Ice Cube	Miguel Tejada
Ashanti	Ja Rule	Nancy Pelosi
Ashlee Simpson	Jamie Foxx	Natasha Bedingfield
Ashton Kutcher	Jay-Z	Orianthi
Avril Lavigne	Jennifer Lopez	Orlando Bloom
Beyoncé	Jessica Simpson	P. Diddy
Blake Lively	J. K. Rowling	Peyton Manning
Bow Wow	Joe Flacco	Pink
Brett Favre	John Legend	Prince William
Britney Spears	Justin Berfield	Queen Latifah
CC Sabathia	Justin Timberlake	Rihanna
Carrie Underwood	Kanye West	**Robert Downey Jr.**
Chris Brown	Kate Hudson	Robert Pattinson
Chris Daughtry	Katy Perry	Ron Howard
Christina Aguilera	Keith Urban	Sean Kingston
Ciara	Kelly Clarkson	Selena
Clay Aiken	Kenny Chesney	Shakira
Cole Hamels	Ke$ha	Shia LaBeouf
Condoleezza Rice	Kristen Stewart	Shontelle Layne
Corbin Bleu	Lady Gaga	Soulja Boy Tell 'Em
Daniel Radcliffe	Lance Armstrong	Stephenie Meyer
David Ortiz	Leona Lewis	Taylor Swift
David Wright	Lil Wayne	T.I.
Derek Jeter	Lindsay Lohan	Timbaland
Drew Brees	Ludacris	Tim McGraw
Eminem	Mariah Carey	Toby Keith
Eve	Mario	Usher
Fergie	Mary J. Blige	Vanessa Anne Hudgens
Flo Rida	Mary-Kate and Ashley Olsen	Zac Efron

Library of Congress Cataloging-in-Publication Data
Leavitt, Amie Jane.
  Robert Downey Jr. / by Amie Jane Leavitt.
    p. cm. — (Blue banner biographies)
  Includes bibliographical references and index.
  Includes filmography.
  ISBN 978-1-61228-056-1 (library bound)
  1. Downey, Robert, 1965– —Juvenile literature. 2. Actors—United States—Biography—Juvenile literature. I. Title.
  PN2287.D548L43 2011
  792.02'8092—dc22
  [B]
                                                                                    2011016781
eBook ISBN: 9781612281834

ABOUT THE AUTHOR: Children's book writer Amie Jane Leavitt graduated from Brigham Young University as an education major and has since taught all grade levels in both private and public schools. She lives with her family in Utah. To find out more about her, visit her web site at http://www.amiejaneleavitt.com.

BLUE BANNER
BIOGRAPHY

Chapter 1
The Man of Iron.. 5

Chapter 2
Acting in His Blood.. 9

Chapter 3
Making His Way in Film.................................... 15

Chapter 4
Public Success, Private Struggles...................... 19

Chapter 5
A Comeback Story... 23

Chronology.. 28

Filmography... 29

Further Reading.. 30

Books.. 30

Works Consulted... 30

On the Internet... 31

Index.. 32

Jon Favreau (right) directed the Iron Man movies starring Robert Downey Jr. (left). Favreau believed Downey was right for the Iron Man role from the first time he saw him audition — but the studio executives at Marvel originally thought differently.

The Man of Iron

*F*or most people in the glitzy beach town of Santa Monica, California, it was just another beautiful early summer evening along the coast. But for Robert Downey Jr., it was the day his career took a giant leap forward. May 2, 2008, was the day *Iron Man* opened in theaters nationwide.

"It's Friday evening, and we're all in a side room at a restaurant in Santa Monica," he recalled to an *Entertainment Weekly* reporter about the night he and his associates waited to see how the film had done in theaters. Throughout the night, they received calls telling them approximately how many millions of dollars in tickets had been sold throughout the country. "And every few minutes the estimates go up," he recalled. " 'The estimate is now 77! The estimate is now 87! The estimate is now 100!' And I'm going crazy because I've had 25 Cokes and three cappuccinos. I'm like, 'Come on, give me another lucky seven!' "

The excitement kept building as the numbers rose higher throughout the weekend. Ten days later, Downey and *Iron Man* director Jon Favreau were invited to have dinner with Paramount executives. "Jon and I give each other a look, like we were made men or something," Downey continued. The executives proudly told them that *Iron Man* had done even better than they had hoped. It had grossed $100.7 million that weekend, which made it the largest opening of a superhero film since *Spider-Man* in 2002.

That was it. "*Iron Man* had put us in the game," Downey said, beaming.

Even though Downey had already been in more than 50 films, he had never been in a blockbuster — one that brings in big bucks at the box office. All that changed when he secured the lead role of Tony Stark in *Iron Man*. As soon as he heard that Paramount Pictures was planning to produce the film, he knew he had to have the role as the superhero. Knowing his one-hour screen test had to be perfect, he rehearsed for three weeks. "He really, really wanted it," his wife, Susan Levin, told *Time* magazine. "Other than *Chaplin*, it's the role he's gone after the hardest."

Downey said in the same interview, "You run [the scene] until your subconscious can cough it up with ease. Then you run it to where, if you were woken up in the middle of the night, you could probably say it backwards. Then you write the whole thing out illegibly and see if you can scream through it as fast as you can, while only having a rough reference of what it is because it's written out like chicken scratch."

Because of Downey's record of making poor personal choices, the producers hesitated to cast him in such an important role. But after they saw his screen test, they knew he was the one they were looking for.

Downey received rave reviews for his performance as the dark superhero. Ann Hornaday of *The Washington Post* wrote, "It's difficult to imagine a better actor-character fit than that between Robert Downey Jr. and Iron Man." David Ansen of *Newsweek* also said, "Many people had a hard time imagining Downey donning superhero garb. [Yet,] in truth, it's hard to

imagine *Iron Man* without him." For *Iron Man*, Downey was nominated for Best Male Performance by the National Movie Awards in the United Kingdom, Best Male Performance by the MTV Movie Awards, and Favorite Superhero by the People's Choice Awards.

With a director as a father, young Robert didn't have to wait very long to get into acting.

Acting in His Blood

On April 4, 1965, Robert John Downey Jr. was born in New York City to Robert John Downey Sr. and Elsie Ford Downey. He joined is sister, Allyson, who was born in 1963.

The Downey family lived in Greenwich Village—an area of Manhattan known for its bohemian lifestyle. This unconventional neighborhood suited Robert Sr.'s career perfectly. He was an underground filmmaker. An underground film is one that does not fit the mainstream mold of regular Hollywood films, either in style, subject matter, or financing. Robert Sr.'s films were considered unusual to some and artistic to others. His films came to be regarded as some of the best underground films produced in New York during the 1960s, but while he was making them, Robert Sr. was just enjoying himself. He told NPR in 2008, "We were just out having fun doing this because we could. . . . Here we were, writers and cameramen saying, 'Hey, you got a script; I got a camera; let's go do something.' "

Robert Downey Sr. was born Robert Elias. In his teens he changed his name to Robert Downey after his stepfather's last name. His mother was Irish Catholic and his father was Russian Jewish.

Elsie Ford Downey, who was of both German and Scottish descent, was an actress, singer, and comedian. She appeared in a number of Robert Sr.'s films, including *Moment to Moment, Greaser's Palace, Pound,* and *Chafed Elbows.* Robert Jr. told *The New York Times* in 1992, "The love of being a performer, I definitely get that from my mom." Later he told *Esquire* magazine that his mother had "dedicated her life to working in accord with my dad's vision," and through his mother, Robert Jr. learned about "throwing yourself into the work—and being very brave and dedicated."

Not only was Elsie featured in Robert Sr.'s films, so were Allyson and Robert Jr. During an *Inside the Actors Studio*

Robert Downey Jr. with his mother, Elsie. She has always been an important part of Robert's life.

Robert with his dad, indie filmmaker Robert Downey Sr., in 2008

interview in 2008, Robert Jr. spoke about performing in his father's productions. He said, "We were certainly convenient. We were right there." By casting his own children, Robert Sr. did not have to audition child actors.

Robert Jr.'s first film appearance was in 1970 when he was five years old. He played the part of a puppy in *Pound*. However, even though he and his sister enjoyed performing, Robert was very different from his older sibling. "[She] was the smart one going to private school," he told *The New York Times* in 1992, "and I was the one who made the company laugh at dinner."

In his early life, Robert was surrounded by filmmakers, actors, and people living the counterculture lifestyle. He told *Inside the Actors Studio*, "It was very natural to have no

In 1976 and 1977, Robert attended Stagedoor Manor, a performing arts summer camp in New York.

interaction with mainstream anything." The Downeys also moved around a lot in those early years. Before Robert turned thirteen, his family had lived in Manhattan and Queens in New York City; London, England; Paris, France; New Mexico; Los Angeles, California; and Woodstock, New York.

By his early teens, his parents decided to divorce. At first, Robert Jr. stayed in New York and lived with his mother, but eventually he made his way out to Los Angeles to live with his father. "[We were living] in this little apartment that wasn't comfortable for either of us," he told Jamie Diamond of *The New York Times*. He enrolled in Samo (Santa Monica High School) and attended classes with such young actors as

Sean Penn, Rob Lowe, Charlie Sheen, and Emilio and Ramon Estevez. Robert and the rest of these actors would eventually be known in Hollywood as the Brat Pack.

When Robert first enrolled in the school, he and Ramon decided to try out for the school play *Oklahoma!* To learn the dance numbers, Robert would go over to the Estevez house in Malibu, and Ramon would teach him how to tap dance. "He would drill me," Robert said during the *Actors Studio* interview. Ramon must have done his job well, because not only did Robert get a part in the play, but he also remembered the routine more than three decades later. During the interview, he performed one of his routines to the great applause of the audience.

In the summer of Robert's junior year, the high school counselor told him he had to attend summer school. Robert opted to quit school altogether to pursue an acting career. He told CNN in 2001, "I consider myself someone who needs to express himself creatively, and acting seems to be the most lucrative and attention-getting way of working it out right now. So, you know, let's see what happens." A short time after leaving Samo High, Robert moved back to New York.

Robert Downey Jr. in high school

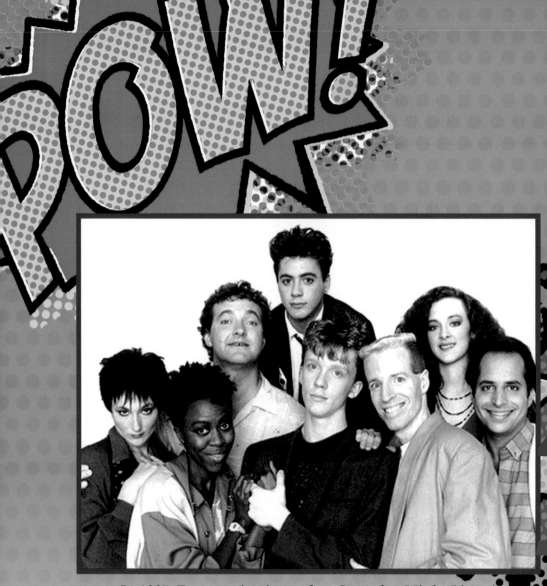

In 1985, Downey (top) acted on **Saturday Night Live** *with (left to right): Nora Dunn, Danitra Vance, Randy Quaid, Anthony Michael Hall, Terry Sweeney, Joan Cusack, and Jon Lovitz.*

Making His Way in Film

*F*or his first two years in New York, Downey lived with his mother and picked up odd jobs while he hoped for his shot in acting. He bused tables at restaurants. He sold shoes at department stores. Finally, in 1983, he secured a role as a high school student in the film *Firstborn*, which was shot on location in New Jersey and New York. While shooting this film, he met his first long-term girlfriend, 18-year-old actress Sarah Jessica Parker.

After finishing *Firstborn*, Downey made his switch to television for just one year. In 1985, he began working as a regular cast member of *Saturday Night Live*. He performed on the show with such comedians as Joan Cusack, Anthony Michael Hall, and Randy Quaid.

Even though Robert was a regular on *Saturday Night Live*, he didn't quit working in film. In 1985, he played the role of Jimmy Parker in *Tuff Turf* and Ian in John Hughes's *Weird Science*. From 1986 to 1989, he performed in ten more movies: *Back to School, America, The Pick-Up Artist, Less Than Zero, Rented Lips, Johnny B. Good, 1969, That's Adequate, True Believer*, and *Chances Are*. Through this decade, he established himself as more than just a Brat Pack twenty-something performer. He was considered by many to be a true artist. Of his 1987 performance in *Less Than Zero*, Janet Maslin of *The New York Times* wrote, "Mr. Downey gives a performance that is desperately moving, with the kind of emotion that comes as a real surprise in these surroundings."

Unfortunately, it was also during these early acting years that Downey's personal life started to unravel. He had been making poor personal choices since his early teens. He stayed out late partying with friends, and he became addicted to drugs. When he became an adult, his drug use increased. It affected every aspect of his personal life, including his relationship with Parker. "He's one of those tortured souls," she told a *Redbook* reporter in 1996. "I just found it incredibly difficult to deal with. . . . I felt so sad, and by the end, I felt exhausted." Downey confessed to the *Huffington Post* in 2008, "[Parker] provided me a home and understanding. She tried to help me. . . . I thought my way was so much cooler than people who were actually building lives and careers. I was in love with Sarah Jessica. [Yet] love clearly was not enough." In 1991, the two broke up for good.

A year later, Robert met and married actress and musician Deborah Falconer. A year after that, their son, Indio Falconer Downey, was born.

Although he still struggled with making good choices in his personal life, Downey somehow managed to achieve continued success in his acting career. In 1990 and 1991, he played in *Air America* with Mel Gibson, *Too Much Sun* directed by his father, and *Soapdish* with Sally Field, Whoopi Goldberg, and Kevin Kline. In 1992, Downey secured the lead role as Charlie Chaplin in Richard Attenborough's biographical film *Chaplin*. He worked hard to get

Downey with his son, Indio

this part and worked even harder to make sure he understood Charlie Chaplin so that he could portray him accurately. He read Chaplin's autobiography and every biographical work that was ever written about him. He watched his films. All of them. Repeatedly. Downey told *Inside the Actors Studio* in 2008, "It was just the ultimate, ultimate education."

While he prepared for the film, Downey also wrote and recorded the song "Smile," which was used in the film and included on the sound track. Of his performance in *Chaplin*, Vincent Canby of *The New York Times* wrote, "He is close to brilliant when he does some of Charlie's early vaudeville and film sketches. His slapstick routines are graceful, witty and, most important, really funny." This performance won him a nomination for an Oscar for Best Actor in a Leading Role in 1993—his first nomination for an Academy Award. He was also nominated for a Golden Globe, and he won Actor of the Year from the London Critics Circle Film Awards and Best Actor from BAFTA (British Academy of Film and Television Arts). On the outside, it seemed as if his life was right on track.

Downey as Chaplin

Robert played Ally McBeal's boyfriend on the television series Ally McBeal (starring Calista Flockhart). Downey liked the idea of playing a "nice guy" in this series.

Public Success, Private Struggles

*I*n 1993, Downey played the lead role of Thomas Reilly in the movie *Heart and Souls.* Critics did not particularly love the film's storyline, but they did enjoy Downey's performance. They said that it reminded them of his performance in *Chaplin* and showed his incredible abilities to pantomime. *Times* movie critic Janet Maslin wrote, "The best thing about the film is the chance to watch [Downey's] uncanny impersonations of his co-stars." For that performance, Downey won a Best Actor Saturn Award from the Academy of Science Fiction, Fantasy & Horror Films. Also in 1993, he played the role of Bill Bush in the Robert Altman film *Short Cuts.* The movie's cast members, which included his wife, Deborah, won a special award at the Golden Globes that year for Best Ensemble Cast.

In the early to mid 1990s, Downey's career looked almost unstoppable. In 1994, he was in three movies; in 1995, he was in four; and in 1996, he was in the action drama *Danger Zone.* However, while things were going phenomenally well in his career, they were not going well in other areas of his life. Downey was still struggling immensely with his addictions, and things were taking a turn for the worse. In 1996, he was arrested numerous times — and most of them were drug related. He was out of control and everyone around him knew it. In July of that year, Judge Lawrence Mira had seen Downey three times in just seven days. Deborah came to the courtroom, in tears, to give her testimony about his behavior. His mother flew in from her home near Pittsburgh to attend the proceedings, and his father drove in from Los Angeles. Even Downey's former manager, Loree Rodkin, spoke about how concerned she was about him. She told *People* magazine, "Every day I look in the newspaper and I think that I am going to read Robert's obituary."

Robert desperately needed help. To be sure he got that help, the court ordered him to enter a 24-hour rehabilitation program at Exodus Recovery Center. After he was released, he would have to have regular drug testing for the next three years.

Despite his brushes with the law, Downey was still able to secure roles in movies during the late 1990s. In 1997, he was in *Two Girls and a Guy* and his father's film *Hugo Pool*. In 1998 and 1999, he was in *The Gingerbread Man, U.S. Marshals, In Dreams, Friends & Lovers, Bowfinger,* and *Black and White*. During these years he still could not stay out of trouble. In 1999, Judge Mira told him, "We tried rehabilitation. It simply has not worked." He ordered Downey to serve three years in prison with two suspended, which meant he served one year. Even though his friends and family were upset by this decision, they hoped it would help him turn his life around.

In 2000, after his time in prison, Downey returned to work. His performance as Terry Crabtree in *Wonder Boys* won him a Screen Idol Award. Later that year, he was in the film *Auto Motives* and was cast in the television series *Ally McBeal*. Downey was credited with significantly boosting the show's ratings. In 2001, he won a Golden Globe and a Screen Actors Guild Award for his performance in that series.

Unfortunately the time he had spent in prison was not enough to help him change. Over the next several years, he continued to allow his drug use to control his life. After one particular arrest, the producers of *Ally McBeal* canceled his contract. Then, in 2001, Deborah filed for divorce. His life kept spiraling further and further out of control.

It became clear that no matter how much help people tried to give him or how much trouble he was in, Downey was never going to change unless he decided to. Finally, he had enough. He told Oprah Winfrey in an interview in 2004, "For me, I just happened to be in a situation the very last time and I said, 'You know what? I don't think I can continue doing this.' And I reached out for help and I ran with it." He committed himself to a live-in treatment program for a year. When he came out, he was on the road to a cleaner life and better choices.

A very happy Robert Downey Jr. chatted with Oprah in 2004 about how glad he was to find peace and health at last.

Robert and Susan Levin Downey enjoy a dance at an Oscar party in 2011.

A Comeback Story

*T*he first decade of the twenty-first century was kind to Robert Downey Jr., both personally and professionally. In 2003, he secured the lead role in the drama *The Singing Detective.* For that movie he was nominated for a Golden Satellite Award for Performance by an Actor. That same year, he was selected to play the role of Pete Graham in *Gothika.* While he didn't receive any awards for his performance in this particular film, he did find something on set that would improve his life immensely: love. He and coproducer Susan Levin started dating, and in 2005 they were married. Downey said of Susan on the *Oprah Winfrey Show* in 2004, "I just feel like she's my best friend and we really get along well. And she also just calls me on everything."

In 2004, Downey decided to try something he had wanted to do since he was nine years old. He had been writing and composing music for as long as he could remember. In some of his films (*Chaplin* and *Heart and Souls*), he had even performed a vocal number or two. He finally decided to record his own album. *The Futurist* was released on Sony Classical in November of that year. His son, Indio, designed the cover art.

From 2004 to 2007, Downey was in a string of films, including *Eros; Game 6; Kiss Kiss Bang Bang; Good Night, and Good Luck; A Guide to Recognizing Your Saints*; Disney's *The Shaggy Dog; A Scanner Darkly; Fur: An Imaginary Portrait of Diane Arbus; Zodiac; Lucky You*; and *Charlie Bartlett*. Susan Downey produced *Kiss Kiss Bang Bang*, and Indio played a minor role. Praise for Downey's performances in these films came by way of award nominations, comments by fellow actors, and opinions by professional critics. In 2005, *Kiss Kiss Bang Bang* costar Val Kilmer told *Entertainment Weekly*, "I think Robert can do anything as an actor. I'm kind of a snob for intelligent actors, and man, he's fast. He's one of the best going in my age group."

Following his immense success with *Iron Man* in 2008, Downey was cast in pal Ben Stiller's film *Tropic Thunder*. This film also did very well at the box office, and Downey's performance in it earned him his second Oscar nomination, this time for Best Supporting Actor. The year 2009 brought him even more success. He played the part of Steve Lopez in the film *The Soloist*. Of his performance in this real-life story, *The*

Downey in Tropic Thunder

Christian Science Monitor said, "Downey doesn't sentimentalize Lopez or soft-pedal his qualms or ambitions. It's a good, tense, live-wire performance." Later that year, Downey performed the lead role in *Sherlock Holmes*. For this performance he was a little nervous, since most people had ideas of what Sherlock Holmes was like, and he couldn't possibly please everyone. He decided to go in with a positive attitude. "Clearly I'm going to do it better than it's ever been done," he told *Entertainment Weekly* in 2009.

And clearly, to many people, he did. Downey received nominations for Teen Choice Awards, MTV Movie Awards, Empire Awards, and Saturn Awards. Critic Michael O'Sullivan of *The Washington Post* said in 2009, "The actor gets one important thing just right. That's a   sense of Holmes as a brilliant misfit, a kind of autistic savant who hears, sees and remembers everything. . . . You can practically feel his senses at work."

In 2010, Downey starred in *Iron Man 2, Love and Distrust,* and *Due Date,* with the sequels to *Sherlock Holmes* and *Iron Man 2* in the works. He and his wife were also planning to direct and produce other films with their company Team Downey.

Downey told *Entertainment Weekly* in 2008, "I'm an actor because I'm crazy about movies." But he is not just an actor. He also has hobbies and interests outside his career. "In my off-screen life, I'm totally into skydiving, martial arts [Wing Chun Kung Fu], military history,"

Downey as Sherlock Holmes

Downey plays Iron Man again in the 2012 movie The Avengers. *His costars in this superhero movie are (left to right) Scarlett Johansson, Chris Hemsworth, Chris Evans, Samuel L. Jackson, Jeremy Renner, Mark Ruffalo, and the film's director, Joss Whedon.*

he said. He used to spend loads of money on expensive clothes, but now he prefers jeans and T-shirts. He enjoys cooking and says that anything with seafood in it is his specialty. He hates big spiders, loves tropical islands (without spiders on them), and enjoys listening to music from such artists as the Doobie Brothers, Bee Gees, Journey, and Van Halen. He also enjoys being a husband and a father.

Robert may have had his set of problems throughout his life, but he made it on to a better path through a lot of hard work and determination. "I see life as a series of challenges and battles that you either win or lose," he told *W* magazine in 2007. In the end, after making a lot of positive choices, he is definitely a winner.

CHRONOLOGY

1965	Robert Downey Jr. is born on April 4 in New York, New York, to Robert Downey Sr. and Elsie Ford Downey.
1970	In his first film, he plays a puppy in his father's movie *Pound*.
1978	His parents divorce. He stays in New York to live with his mother.
1980	He moves to Los Angeles to live with his father. He enrolls at Santa Monica High School.
1982	He quits high school to pursue acting full-time. He returns to live with his mother in New York.
1983	He is cast in his first Hollywood film, *Firstborn*. He meets actress Sarah Jessica Parker and starts a seven-year relationship with her.
1985	He is cast for one year on *Saturday Night Live* and in four films, including *Weird Science* with Anthony Michael Hall.
1987	He is cast as Julian in *Less Than Zero*, a role that many feared was true to his own life.
1991	He and Sarah Jessica Parker end their relationship.
1992	He meets and marries Deborah Falconer. He secures the role of Charlie Chaplin in *Chaplin*. For his performance, he is nominated for an Oscar for Best Actor.
1993	His son with Deborah, Indio Falconer Downey, is born.
1996	He is arrested numerous times for charges relating to substance abuse. The court orders him to a rehabilitation center.
1999	He is ordered to serve three years in the California State Prison, but two are suspended.
2001	Deborah files for a divorce. Robert checks himself into a yearlong live-in drug treatment program.
2002	He completes his rehabilitation program.
2003	He meets Susan Levin on the set of *Gothika*.
2004	He releases his first music album, *The Futurist*, on Sony Classical.
2005	He marries Levin on August 27.
2008	His first blockbuster, *Iron Man*, is released in theaters.
2009	He stars in *The Soloist* and *Sherlock Holmes*.
2010	He stars in *Iron Man 2, Love & Distrust,* and *Due Date*. He and Susan launch their production company, Team Downey.
2011	He reprises his role as Tony Stark/Iron Man in *The Avengers*, set for release in 2012.

28

FILMOGRAPHY

2012	*The Avengers*	1997	*Hugo Pool*
2011	*Sherlock Holmes: A Game of Shadows*		*Two Girls and a Guy*
			One Night Stand
2010	*Due Date*	1996	*Danger Zone*
	Love & Distrust (video)	1995	*Restoration*
	Iron Man 2		*Home for the Holidays*
2009	*Sherlock Holmes*		*Richard III*
	The Soloist	1994	*Only You*
2008	*Tropic Thunder*		*Natural Born Killers*
	Iron Man		*Hail Caesar*
2007	*Charlie Bartlett*	1993	*Short Cuts*
	Lucky You		*Heart and Souls*
	Zodiac	1992	*Chaplin*
2006	*Fur: An Imaginary Portrait of Diane Arbus*	1991	*Soapdish*
		1990	*Too Much Sun*
	A Scanner Darkly		*Air America*
	The Shaggy Dog	1989	*Chances Are*
	A Guide to Recognizing Your Saints		*True Believer*
			That's Adequate
2005	*Good Night, and Good Luck*	1988	*1969*
			Rented Lips
	Kiss Kiss Bang Bang		*Johnny Be Good*
	Game 6	1987	*Less Than Zero*
2004	*Eros*		*The Pick-Up Artist*
2003	*Gothika*	1986	*America*
	The Singing Detective		*Back to School*
2000–2002	*Ally McBeal* (TV series)	1985–1986	*Saturday Night Live* (TV series)
2000	*Wonder Boys*		
1999	*Black and White*	1985	*Mussolini: The Untold Story* (TV mini-series)
	Bowfinger		
	Friends & Lovers		*Weird Science*
	In Dreams		*Tuff Turf*
1998	*U.S. Marshals*	1984	*Firstborn*
	The Gingerbread Man	1983	*Baby It's You*
		1970	*Pound*

FURTHER READING

Books

Doyle, Sir Arthur Conan. *Classic Starts: The Adventures of Sherlock Holmes.* New York: Sterling, 2005.

Fleischman, Sid. *Sir Charlie: Chaplin, the Funniest Man in the World.* New York: Green Willow Books, 2010.

Huelin, Jodi. *Iron Man 2: Iron Man Fights Back.* New York: LB Kids, 2010.

Works Consulted

Actors Studio, The. *Robert Downey Jr. – Inside The Actors Studio* Pt. 1, 2008. http://www.youtube.com/watch?v=6ZzKGak0jYI

Ansen, David. "Putting the Irony in 'Iron Man.' " *Newsweek,* May 1, 2008. http://www.newsweek.com/2008/04/30/putting-the-irony-in-iron-man.html#

Canby, Vincent. "Review/Film; Robert Downey Jr. in Charlie Chaplin Life Story." *The New York Times,* December 25, 1992. http://www.nytimes.com/1992/12/25/movies/review-film-robert-downey-jr-in-charlie-chaplin-life-story.html

"The Comeback Kid." *The Oprah Winfrey Show,* November 23, 2004. http://www.oprah.com/oprahshow/The-Comeback-Kid/1.

Diamond, Jamie. "FILM; Robert Downey Jr. Is Chaplin (on Screen) and a Child (Off)." *The New York Times,* December 20, 1992. http://query.nytimes.com/gst/fullpage.html?res=9E0CE2DB1039F933A15751C1A964958260

Gliatto, Tom, and Ken Baker. "Hitting Bottom." *People,* August 19, 1996, Vol. 46, Issue 8, p. 70.

Horn, John, and Ana Figueroa. "Robert Downey Jr. Takes One Day at a Time." *Newsweek,* February 12, 2001, Vol. 137, Issue 7, p. 52.

Hornaday, Ann. " 'Iron Man' Shows Strength of Character." *The Washington Post,* May 2, 2008. http://www.washingtonpost.com/wp-dyn/content/article/2008/05/01/AR2008050103883.html?nav=rss_print/style

Jensen, Jeff. "Iron Man." *Entertainment Weekly,* April 25, 2008, Issue 988/989, pp. 38–41.

Karr, Rick. "Robert Downey Sr., Underground and Off the Cuff." *NPR,* September 29, 2008. http://www.npr.org/templates/story/story.php?storyId=94926945

Keegan, Rebecca Winters. "Why Is This Man Smiling?" *Time International* (South Pacific Edition), April 28, 2008, Issue 16, pp. 55–57.

Maslin, Janet. "Film: 'Less Than Zero,' Young Lives." *The New York Times,* November 6, 1987. http://query.nytimes.com/gst/fullpage.html?res=9B0DE4DA1239F935A35752C1A961948260

——. "*Heart and Souls* (1993) Reviews/Film; A Yuppie Haunted (Really) by Other People's Problems." *The New York Times,* August 13, 1993. http://movies.nytimes.com/movie/review?res=9F0CE1DF1F38F930A2575BC0A965958260

Nashawaty, Chris. "Marathon Man." *Entertainment Weekly,* October 28, 2005, Issue 847, pp. 28–34.

FURTHER READING

O'Sullivan, Michael. "Robert Downey Jr.'s 'Sherlock Holmes' Isn't for the Doyle Faithful." *The Washington Post,* December 25, 2009. http://www.washingtonpost.com/gog/movies/sherlock-holmes,1158961/critic-review.html

"Profiles of Robert Downey Jr., Morgan Freeman, Rufus Wainwright." *CNN People in the News,* transcript, aired August 17, 2002. http://edition.cnn.com/TRANSCRIPTS/0208/17/pitn.00.html

Raab, Scott. "Robert Downey Jr.: The Second Greatest Actor in the World." *Esquire,* November 10, 2009. http://www.esquire.com/features/robert-downey-jr-interview-1209

Ranier, Peter. "Review: 'The Soloist'." *Christian Science Monitor,* April 24, 2009. http://www.csmonitor.com/The-Culture/Movies/2009/0424/p17s02-almo.html

"Robert Downey Jr. on Dating Sarah Jessica Parker, Parenting and Drug Use." *Huffington Post,* April 16, 2008. http://www.huffingtonpost.com/2008/04/16/robert-downey-jr-on-datin_n_97012.html

Rottenberg, Josh. "Robert Downey Jr." *Entertainment Weekly,* November 27, 2009, Issue 1077, pp. 32–37.

Svetkey, Benjamin. "No. 1 Entertainer of the Year: Robert Downey Jr." *Entertainment Weekly,* November 21, 2008, Issue 1021/1022, pp. 26–32.

Weinraub, Bernard. "Sarah Jessica Parker on Stardom, Dating (Nick Cage, JFK Jr., Matthew Broderick), and the Baby She'd Love to Have." *Redbook,* July 1996, Vol. 187, Issue 3, p. 54.

West, Kevin. "Robert Downey, Jr. Call Him Mr. Clean." *W Magazine,* March 2007. http://www.wmagazine.com/celebrities/2007/03/robert_downey_jr#ixzz18OR938WB

On the Internet
Marvel Comics: Iron Man
    http://marvel.com/universe/Iron_Man_(Anthony_Stark)
Robert Downey Jr. Music
    http://www.robertdowneyjrmusic.com
Sherlock Holmes Website
    http://www.sherlockholmesonline.org/

INDEX

Ally McBeal 18, 20–21

Avengers, The 26

Brat Pack 13, 16

Chaplin 16–17, 19, 23

Chaplin, Charlie 16–17

Cusak, Joan 14, 15

Downey, Allyson (sister) 9, 10–11

Downey, Elsie Ford (mother) 9–11, 12, 20

Downey, Indio Falconer (son) 16, 24

Downey, Robert, Jr.
   acting technique 6, 17
   awards 7, 17, 19, 20, 23, 24, 25
   birth of 9
   childhood of 8, 9–13
   divorce 21
   drug use 16, 19–21
   education 12, 13, 17
   high school years of 13
   hobbies of 25–26
   music of 17, 23–24

Downey, Robert, Sr. (father) 8, 9–11, 12, 16, 20

Downey, Susan Levin (second wife) 6, 22, 23, 24, 25

Estevez, Emilio 13

Estevez, Ramon 13

Falconer, Deborah (first wife) 16, 19, 20, 21

Favreau, Jon 4, 5

Firstborn 15

Flockhart, Calista 18

Foxx, Jamie 7

Futurist, The (album) 23

Hall, Anthony Michael 14, 15

Heart and Souls 19, 23

Iron Man 4, 5–7, 24, 25, 26–27

Kilmer, Val 24

Less Than Zero 15, 16

Levin, Susan (*see* Susan Levin Downey)

Lowe, Rob 13

Mira, Lawrence 20

MTV Movie Awards 7, 25

Parker, Sarah Jessica 15–16

Penn, Sean 13

People's Choice Awards 7

Pound 10, 11

Quaid, Randy 14, 15

Rodkin, Loree 20

Santa Monica High School 12, 13

Saturday Night Live 14, 15

Sheen, Charlie 13

Sherlock Holmes 25

Short Cuts 19

Soloist, The 24–25

Stagedoor Manor 12

Stiller, Ben 24

Tropic Thunder 24

Tuff Turf 15

Weird Science 15

Winfrey, Oprah 21, 23

Wonder Boys 20